Portrait of the Settle–Carlisle

Uniform with this volume:
SETTLE–CARLISLE IN COLOUR

Other Dalesman books on the line and its branches:
LIFE ON THE SETTLE–CARLISLE RAILWAY
SETTLE TO CARLISLE: A Railway over the Pennines
THE WENSLEYDALE RAILWAY

Portrait of the Settle–Carlisle

compiled by David Joy

Dalesman Books
1984

The Dalesman Publishing Company Ltd.,
Clapham, via Lancaster LA2 8EB
First published 1984

ISBN: 0 85206 806 9

Printed in Great Britain by Fretwell & Brian Ltd.,
Healey Works, Goulbourne Street, Keighley, West Yorkshire

Contents

Cover photographs:

Front: A3 No. 4472 *Flying Scotsman* crosses Dent Head viaduct with the up Cumbrian Mountain Pullman, July 1983. *(Robert Leslie)*

Back: Class 47 No. 47481 at Ribblehead with a diverted Glasgow–Paddington express, May 1984. *(Peter J. Robinson)*

Map on page 12 by Peter W. Robinson. Gradient profile by A. Haigh.
The assistance of Peter Fox in the preparation of Section 4 is gratefully acknowledged.

Introduction

YET another book on the Settle to Carlisle railway surely calls for a few words of explanation. The prime purpose of this work is as a sequel and companion to *Settle–Carlisle in Colour,* which met with almost overwhelming enthusiasm when published in 1983. It was the first serious attempt to portray the atmosphere, character and motive power of the route in other than monochrome. As O. S. Nock commented in his foreword: 'The wonderful North Country atmosphere that I grew to love when I was at Giggleswick simply shines out from these pages. When the wide prospects of North Ribblesdale, Denthead and Mallerstang Common are rendered in all the glory of their natural colouring, to set off the "spit and polish" of lovingly cleaned locomotives, it is indeed time to rejoice.'

This time the approach is slightly different. Instead of taking the form of a journey up the line, the colour photographs are grouped into three broad time-spans — the true steam age which ended in 1968, the diesel era and finally the return of steam from 1978. An additional section of black & white photographs takes the time-scale back to LMS days and looks at now-vanished features of the route.

It is freely admitted that Settle & Carlisle diehards will not learn a great deal from the accompanying text, for in truth there is little new to be said about this much-chronicled subject. But there are many newcomers to the fold who wish to know more about this incredible main line over the Pennines; it is for them that the content — and especially the tabular detail — has been devised, so that this work forms both a colour album and a concise handbook.

For in the twelve months since the publication of *Settle–Carlisle in Colour,* an immense amount has happened as is summarised in the first section of this book. British Rail has finally come clean and announced its intention to withdraw passenger services. The result has been a quite unparalleled wave of opposition. Saving the Settle–Carlisle has ceased to be merely the avowed aim of railway enthusiasts and has instead become a national cause. There has been massive media coverage and much heady talk of consortiums, feasibility studies, leisure complexes and privatisation. In true British fashion, entrenched positions have been assumed and battle lines drawn. The Settle & Carlisle, misconceived at birth, ignored for the greater part of its existence and now hovering on the brink of extinction, is suddenly receiving more attention than at any time in its life.

— *David Joy,*
October 1984

1.

“Closure by Stealth”

"Closure by Stealth"

"RIBBLEHEAD Viaduct is rapidly coming to the end of its life. The degree of deterioration has accelerated rapidly in the last few years. Three years might see it through, five years or thereabouts would be the limit." The words were those of Alan King, Civil Engineer for British Rail's Preston Division. Uttered early in 1981, they marked the start of a saga which has been of quite compelling drama and fascination. For on the face of it they provided the trump card to enable BR to divest itself of an economic thorn in the flesh: a main-line railway which in 72 miles managed to serve not a single place of real importance.

The next move came later the same year when it was announced that the Settle & Carlisle's Inter-City service — comprising three Nottingham–Glasgow trains each way daily — was to be diverted via Manchester and Preston and replaced by two Leeds–Carlisle 'locals'. British Rail insisted it was 'entirely a commercial decision', but there were many allegations of 'dirty tricks' and 'closure by stealth'. Leaked documents subsequently proved that this was exactly what was happening: a deliberate policy was being pursued of removing traffic so that it could be claimed the line was not needed. Surely, the argument ran, there could be no case for replacing Ribblehead viaduct at a cost approaching £6 million if the railway was not essential as a through route.

These moves were a factor leading to the formation of the Friends of the Settle–Carlisle Line, but despite their protests and those of the railway unions, Members of Parliament and the Transport Users' Consultative Committee (TUCC), the proposed changes were implemented at the start of the new timetable in May 1982. Buffet car expresses were replaced by pathetic four-coach formations running to schedules that seemed to have been designed to be as slow and inconvenient as possible.

It took only another twelve months for the planned run-down to be completed with the diversion of all through freight traffic to other routes, a move that created extra mileage and caused high-speed services to be disrupted while Settle & Carlisle signalmen sat for hours on end without a train in sight. Paranoia set in with British Rail determined at all costs to retain its stance that the tracks over Ais Gill were surplus to requirements. When the new freight arrangements were introduced, a goods that had got as far as Skipton was actually turned back! Light engines northbound for Carlisle were sent round via Carnforth and the edict went out that the line was not to be used for diversionary purposes. For many winters it had been the practice on Sundays for West Coast main line services to be routed over the Settle & Carlisle in the morning and early afternoon so that essential engineering work could take place. This came to an end with the winter 1984/5 timetable, prepared in 1983, which revealed a sorry state of affairs. Virtually the whole of Cumbria became a railway desert, passengers southbound from Carlisle having to face a 2½ hour bus journey to Preston or wait until the first train of the day to Euston at the decidedly late hour of 3.45pm. Northbound, the morning Liverpool–Glasgow service made a massive detour via

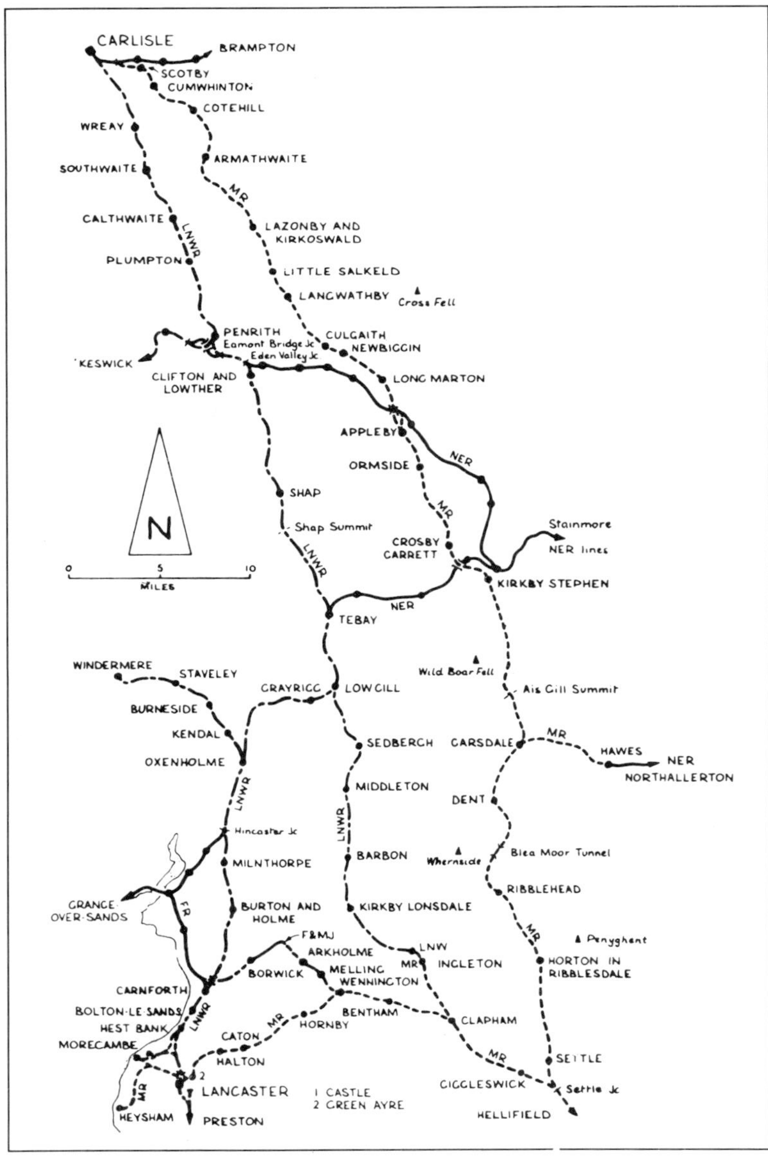

York and Newcastle.

In many ways, British Rail overdid it. Had the whole approach looked rather less deceitful, the opposition to the inevitable closure announcement in August 1983 might not have been quite so determined. BR's case was that withdrawal of passenger services, enabling the tracks to be lifted north of Ribblehead quarry and south of Appleby, would bring a net annual saving of £1.5 million and a total saving on capital expenditure of £6.7 million — mainly on Ribblehead viaduct. Hardly had these figures been released than there was a further leaking of documents, showing that BR had 'adjusted' the budget by increasing the cost of diesel fuels by 250 per cent and diesel locomotive maintenance by a staggering 450 per cent.

The next step was for British Rail to publish a formal closure notice, giving objectors six weeks to make representations to the TUCC at York or Manchester. This it did in December 1983, by a supreme irony on the same day that it was forced to divert West Coast main line services over the route as the result of a severe derailment. It was but the first of several embarrassments, for under the threat of legal action it was conceded that users of Dales Rail and steam-hauled excursions were also eligible to object and therefore the notices were re-issued. Then it was pointed out that the Newcastle TUCC could also hear objections — and so the whole procedure had to be gone through for a third time!

Arguably, the whole concept of TUCC hearings is outmoded. In theory they are only empowered to listen to cases of hardship — a state of being that is far more difficult to substantiate than

The Settle–Carlisle railway and associated lines.

By the time the 9.7am from Leeds had arrived at Settle to begin the 30-mile run which is one of the most spectacular in England, there were many already convinced that the people running British Rail had the economic vision of a transport cafe owner and the souls of philistines.

— The Guardian, August 1983 (the month of the closure announcement)

The line is a tribute to Victorian engineering skills and is now undeniably part of our National Heritage. This can only remain the case if it is retained as a working railway. The Settle–Carlisle Railway has sometimes been referred to as the line that should not have been built. Even if that had been true, now is clearly not the time to abandon it. The line meets important social needs and is coming into its own as an important tourist and recreational attraction. We remain fully committed to the retention of the Settle–Carlisle Railway.

— Statement by the commissioning authorities on publication of the PEIDA report (August 1984)

The Settle to Carlisle railway is a lifeline for the communities in the dales along its route and its closure would be a disaster for them. It would also destroy Dalesrail, a vital link for ramblers to the National Park and one of the most important and successful public transport experiments in the country. It would be a national disgrace for the Settle–Carlisle line to be closed because neither British Rail nor the government can find the relatively paltry sum that is needed to maintain it.

— Alan Mattingly, Secretary, Ramblers' Association (September 1984)

mere inconvenience. In normal circumstances the only objectors who have any chance of being effective are daily commuters — and such a species does not really exist on the Settle & Carlisle. Hearings also tend to be one-sided in that British Rail alone has all the figures, assembled by such convoluted accounting methods that it is virtually impossible to refute them.

In order to challenge the BR case, Cumbria County Council took the initiative in bringing together the relevant local authorities and tourist boards to sponsor a £30,000 independent report on the future of the line by the planning and economic consultants PEIDA. Published in the summer of 1984 and summarised below, it put the whole, by now emotive, Settle & Carlisle debate on a factual footing. Yet in several ways it fudged the real issues. It was rather more optimistic about Ribblehead viaduct, and yet failed to make a detailed appraisal of the various repair options. It conceded that closure would impose a high social cost but neither analysed this in detail nor made its own assessment of the figures claimed by BR. It showed

The PEIDA Report

A summary of the findings of the 1984 report by planning and economic consultants PEIDA, an independent inquiry commissioned by 17 regional councils and tourist authorities in the north of England:

1. In 1983 Britisih Rail announced its intention to withdraw all passenger services between Settle and Carlisle and to close Settle and Appleby stations, retaining only those sections north of Appleby and south of Ribblehead for local freight traffic.

2. In effect, the 1983 statement was the public confirmation of a decision dating back to at least 1980. Since the 1970s, BR has been transferring or discontinuing services over the Settle and Carlisle line and since 1980 it has carried through only the most minimum level of maintenance of track and capital structures.

3. Even with 'good husbandry' the Settle and Carlisle line would require substantial capital investment to ensure its continued operation. However, given the age of the structures on the line and the severe weather conditions to which they are exposed, BR's policy of minimal maintenance has added materially to the capital investment now required for continued operation.

4. The most serious cause of deterioration of the structures has been the ingress of water, in many cases through waterproofing membranes which are no longer effective. The problem has been recognised by BR but finance has not been provided to replace the waterprooofing.

5. It is not possible to make a meaningful calculation of the difference between the level of investment now required for continued operation and the level of investment which might have been required if 'good husbandry' had been observed. Nonetheless, the difference is clearly material. The report describes the policy of BR as one of 'wanton neglect' and that phrase is carefully chosen. The action of BR has materially advanced the case for closure and calls into question the efficacy of the machinery presently used to consider closure.

6. With the strong reservation noted in (5) above, the study proceeded by estimating the capital expenditure now required, given the existing condition of the track and capital structures. Public attention has concentrated on the condition of Ribblehead viaduct. Detailed examination confirms its poor state of repair but it also demonstrates a much wider problem involving the track and many other structures. It should be noted that available information indicates that there is sufficient capacity on the West Coast Main Line to accommodate any foreseeable increase in passenger and freight traffic.

7. On the basis of single track operation, the capital and maintenance costs for structures of operating the line for 20 years is estimated at £15.559 million in current (1984) prices, equivalent to £12.781 million if that stream of expenditure is discounted (at 5%) to present value terms. In addition, the present value cost for track capital and maintenance and signalling costs is estimated to be £5.731 million.

that it would cost virtually as much to close the line as to keep it open with enhanced revenue, and yet finally left the ball firmly in the government's court by stating that it would be unrealistic for BR to maintain existing operations in view of the high financial considerations. Not surprisingly, the report was seen by both British Rail and the closure opponents as vindicating their case.

In the meantime the opposing forces had been preparing for the coming fray. The word 'project' took on a new and negative meaning when British Rail appointed a Project Manager to oversee the closure of the line. The matter was debated in Parliament, with David Mitchell, junior transport minister, subsequently making a fact-finding trip in a special train. In order to achieve better co-ordination, the Friends joined with Transport 2000 and the Railway Development Society to form the Settle–Carlisle Railway Joint Action Committee, which late in 1984 broke new ground in the area of opposition to rail closures by deciding to become a limited company with full-time staff and a proposed annual budget of £55.000.

8. The option costed in (7) assumes continued operation of the line for local services, limited through traffic and use as a diversionary route, with an increased emphasis on improving local services and steam excursions.

9. Existing BR estimates of revenue from the Settle and Carlisle line appear unduly conservative and more effective marketing of the line for local services, Dales Rail and steam excursions could improve future income. However, it is unlikely that future revenue would cover operating costs, and it is estimated that the annual operating deficit might be in excess of £100,000 per annum at 1984 prices, even assuming enhanced revenue. This is equivalent to a further deficit of £1.373 million in present value terms to be added to the deficit identified in (6) above.

10. Under the Railways Act (1974) government payments are made to BR for complying with a 'Public Service Obligation' (PSO) to maintain provincial rail services which are not viable. So long as the PSO is laid upon BR, the Settle and Carlisle line should be regarded as a legitimate candidate for public subsidy. However, on a *pro rata* to passenger miles basis, the application of the PSO to the Settle and Carlisle line would only cover some one-third of the deficit identified above.

11. Various options for developing the line for tourist purposes were considered. The line has potential for such development but experience in the rest of the UK demonstrates that there would be considerable difficulty in obtaining a positive net financial contribution from such an operation, particularly given the terrain and length of the line. On optimistic assumptions, additional intensive tourist use of the line might yield an excess of revenue over operating costs of some £2.1 million in present value terms over a 20 year period. Such operation would require extensive grant and support to defray the investment needs identified in (6).

12. The heavy capital and maintenance expenditures required for track and structures, and the possibility of continued operating losses, rule out any prospect of privatisation. Continued operation depends on BR's willingness to finance the capital costs and operating losses or alternative sources of private donations and/or grant income. As far as the latter alternative is concerned, a vigorous fund-raising campaign might yield an estimated £1.6–4.2 million, although the actual outcome would probably be toward the lower end of that range and could only be achieved over a period of a few years.

13. Consideration of a proposal for line closure cannot finally depend on the costs and benefits to the line operator, but rather should rest on the costs and benefits which accrue to society as a whole. These wider aspects are considered through a cost-benefit appraisal. This does not reach a very clear-cut result, the outcome depending on a number of key assumptions which are clearly open to challenge.

14. While the cost-benefit appraisal is marginal, it does demonstrate that the costs of closure would be substantial. Moreover, other less tangible benefits exist which would be lost by closure.

15. There is no effective alternative to the continued operation of the line by BR. It would be unrealistic , however, to expect BR to meet the financial cost imposed by continued operation and such operation is only likely to be secured by specific support from central government.

The campaign had taken off, which meant that people were flocking from far and wide to make what they feared would be a last journey over the line. The regular trains gradually grew in length until in the summer of 1984 they extended to eleven coaches — and even then it was often standing-room only. The number of objections also steadily increased until they passed the 20,000 mark — a total quite without precedent.

In October 1984, in the face of this massive public response, there were signs of a change in British Rail strategy. Many national newspapers claimed that BR was seeking a way of permanently reprieving the line by the use of Common Market funds. It was confirmed that a £100,000 civil engineering programme, including belated replacement of the waterproof decking for Ribblehead viaduct, had been put in hand, and that a marketing campaign to increase the use and leisure-potential of the route was being planned.

Whether this was a ploy to dilute opposition, or a recognition that closure processes could take years rather than months and even then might not succeed, is an open question. By the time the various hearings are over, it is more than possible that the transport minister will be in the unenviable position of having to make a political decision on the line's fate during the run-up to a general election. Local railwaymen cynically point out that the Settle & Carlisle runs through three marginal constituencies!

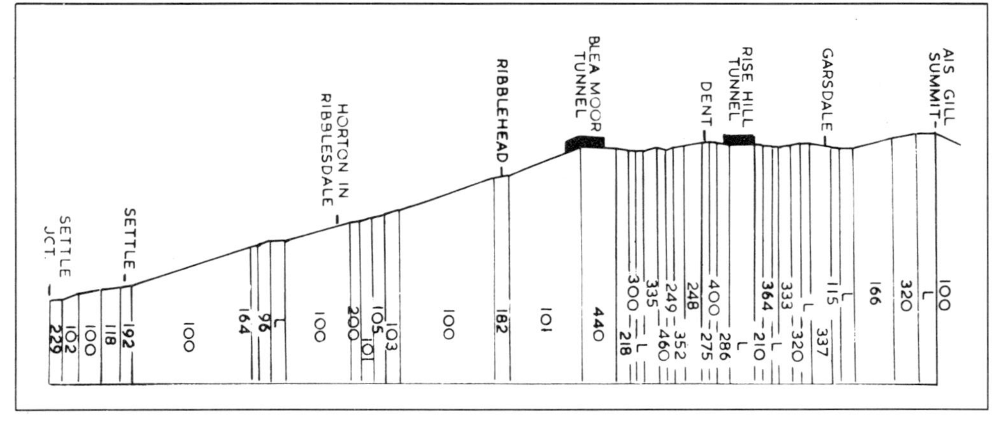

Gradient profile — Settle Junction to Ais Gill.

Scene near Cotehill showing typical Settle & Carlisle train formation of LMS days — double-headed by 2P 4–4–0 No. 521 and a 'Jubilee'. ***(E. E. Smith)***

The Changing Scene

Opposite page.

Top: Appleby station in 1905. *(L&GRP)*

Bottom, left: Ais Gill shortly after the erection of new summit signboards in 1953. *(British Rail)*

Bottom, right: Ribblehead station, prior to demolition of the up platform. *(W. R. Mitchell)*

This page.

Top: Horton-in-Ribblesdale station, 1952. *(L&GRP)*

Bottom, left: Snow clearance at Dent in the winter of 1962–3. *(Isaac Hailwood)*

Bottom, right: North portal of Armathwaite tunnel in LMS times. *(D. Ibbotson)*

Focus on Garsdale

Opposite page.

Top: Hawes Junction — as the station was then known — in 1905. ***(L&GRP)***

Bottom, left: The unique stockaded turntable. ***(Real Photographs)***

Bottom, right: The highest watertroughs in the world just south of the station. ***(Geoffrey G. Hoare)***

This page.

Top: 5MT No. 45012 on an up freight, February 1954. ***(Real Photographs)***

Bottom, left: G5 No. 67314 leaves on the Hawes branch train. ***(J. W. Armstrong)***

Bottom, right: 'Britannia' No. 70002 ***Geoffrey Chaucer*** **heads north over Dandry Mire viaduct, June 1965.** ***(Derek Cross)***

The Hawes–Hellifield afternoon stopping train — nicknamed "Bonny Face" — crosses Dent Head viaduct in charge of an Ivatt 2–6–2T. This service was withdrawn in 1959 on closure of the Hawes branch. *(J. F. Riley)*

Shadows gather over Blea Moor as 'Jubilee' No. 45657 *Tyrwhitt* pounds north with the London St. Pancras–Edinburgh Waverley express at Easter 1954. *(J. F. Riley)*

An ex-works 8F 2–8–0 No. 48399 of Holbeck shed drifts into Appleby with a down freight.
(Peter Walton)

'Scot' 4–6–0 No. 46115 *Scots Guardsman* pauses at Appleby station on the 5.42pm stopping service to Bradford Forster Square. ***(Peter Walton)***

2.

Main Line through the Mountains

Main Line through the Mountains

THE Settle–Carlisle railway is unique. There is nowhere else in the world where a potentially high-speed main line has been driven across such difficult country. Nothing could be more unexpected on the harsh tops of the Pennines than this one-time trunk route nudging the clouds as it sweeps with supreme self-confidence over deep ravines, through rugged mountains and along precipitous ledges. A tour de force of both the Midland Railway and Victorian engineering, it displays panache, style and striking visual unity. And yet this product of the high noon of inter-company hostility was never intended!

Its origins go back to the mid 1850s when the Derby-based Midland Railway decided to pursue an expansionist policy and take on the established Anglo–Scottish routes of the East and West Coast partners. Gradually by means of extensions and mergers it reached south towards London and also north from Leeds through Skipton and Settle to the then remote village of Ingleton on the borders of the West Riding and Lancashire. Here from 1861 it exchanged traffic in an atmosphere of mutual distrust with its arch-rival the London & North Western Railway, the dominant partner in the West Coast alliance. The two companies had separate stations at either end of the viaduct over the Greta, passengers being turfed out of the train and forced to trudge through the township only to see the so-called 'connection' puffing away into the distance.

It was an intolerable situation for the Midland which in a matter of months let it be known that it proposed to build its own main line over the Pennines to Carlisle where it could link up with Scottish companies that were equally antagonistic towards the West Coast partners. A final attempt to agree joint use of existing London & North Western tracks from Ingleton to the 'Border City' collapsed, and in 1866 the Midland obtained powers to spend almost £2¼ million on its brave new route to Scotland. Just two years later the project appeared dead; times were getting harder, the 'Premier Line' was regretting its previous intractability and so agreement between the two rivals was finally reached. The Midland trotted back to Parliament for sanction to abandon its proposed railway over the fells — and promptly came unstuck. Its allies in both England and Scotland, ecstatic at the prospect of a line which would at last enable them to be free from dependence on the domineering London & North Western, lobbied and petitioned to such effect that the abandonment Bill was thrown out. From this moment the Midland was in the extraordinary position of having to construct a main line it no longer wanted. It is to its everlasting credit that it did not take pique and build to the poorest and cheapest standards possible but instead thrust a quite superlative railway through some of the bleakest and most inhospitable country in Britain.

The Settle & Carlisle was the last of the great trunk routes to be almost wholly dependent on the traditional navvy for its creation. At the peak of construction in the summer of 1871 the work-force numbered almost 7,000. Mechanical aids included tramways with attendant locomotives, tip-wagons, fixed steam engines at the heads of tunnel shafts and mobile cranes for erecting the viaducts. Dynamite, then a novelty, was brought by road from Newcastle and Carlisle. Over 500 horses were also employed by the various contractors.

On the windswept and treeless upper section of the route, which had hitherto remained almost immune from the influence of human settlement, a major problem was the provision of accommodation for the navvies. Shanty towns appeared at many places between Settle and Appleby, the largest and most famous being that at Batty Green, Ribblehead, which in its often overcrowded and rat-infested wooden huts housed a maximum of 2,000 men, women and children, and a vast assortment of domestic animals. Reminiscent of something out of the American Mid-West, this was a complete community which boasted shops, an abundance of pubs, a hospital, post office, bakery, slaughterhouse, library, mission house and day and Sunday schools, as well as stables, stores, workshops, a brickworks and a sawmill. The contractors had to offer high wages and short-time working in order to tempt men to wrestle with the bog and boulder clay of the Pennines, but even so, many navvies drifted away in search of an easier livelihood and by 1871 the turnover had reached 73 per cent annually. In a two-pronged approach to maintaining harmony, both scripture readers and policemen were appointed to watch over the work-force with its potentially explosive mixture of English, Irish and Scots. There were numerous isolated incidents such as the 'dreadful commotion' at Armathwaite one pay-day which culminated in an Irishman being beaten to death and a muster of a hundred English navvies coming into confrontation with the armed constabulary. Many deaths resulted from inebriation and wild living, as well as from outbreaks of smallpox, and the tiny graveyards at Chapel-le-Dale church, west of Batty Green, and at Cowgill in Dentdale had to be extended.

In the autumn of 1871 the contractor responsible for the southern section of the line from Settle to Dent Head got into financial difficulties. The Midland took over the work itself, and now became directly aware of the almost superhuman problems involved in building a railway through such challenging countryside. The extremes of the local climate, with its howling gales, 'horizontal' blizzards, persistent mists and seemingly incessant rainfall, proved too much on top of the delays already caused by a fickle labour force. By 1873, when the line should have been completed, only 3¾ miles were open for mineral traffic. A further frustrating two years elapsed before through freight services commenced in August 1875, and even then part of the line was still single track. Only when the earthworks had fully consolidated did the passenger opening take place without official ceremony on 1 May 1876. The Midland had at long last realised its ambition of having an independent Anglo–Scottish route and could look forward to the future with confidence.

The first fifteen miles of the Settle & Carlisle consist of virtually unbroken climbing at 1 in 100 up Ribblesdale to Blea Moor, this stretch having been nicknamed the 'Long Drag' by generations of perspiring enginemen. Almost at the head of the climb is Ribblehead station, notorious for its climatic extremes and for many years an official meteorological reporting point. Just beyond is the line's outstanding feature, the ¼-mile long and majestically curved Ribblehead viaduct with its 24 arches reaching a maximum height of over 100ft above the boggy moorland. For the next fifteen miles the route becomes more undulating but never drops below the 1000ft contour. It curves eastwards to enter the 1½ mile Blea Moor tunnel, piercing an outlier of the 2,414ft peak of Whernside, and emerges to run on a ledge high above green and winding Dentdale. Extensive views from viaducts at Dent Head and Arten Gill precede the approach to Dent station, at 1,145ft the highest on an English main line and

Ribblehead viaduct, absolutely alone in a wilderness of rough windblown moorland, with 2,414ft. Whernside as a backcloth, is one of the most dramatically situated engineering works in England. It spans Batty Moss, once a navvy settlement, now utterly deserted. During construction this and other places like it were roaring shanty towns where the ruddy-faced navvies, dressed in flamboyant clothing and with outlandish nicknames to match, raised their families and laboured like titans on the last of the great English railways to be built by brawn.

— Peter E. Baughan, "Centenary of the Long Drag" (1976)

The two horrors of the Settle and Carlisle were bog and boulder clay. A man would strike his pick in what had up to then proved to be soft clay, strike a boulder underneath almost as hard as iron, and so shake his arms and body that he would fling down his tools disgusted, ask for his money and go off. The men trod on wet heather and sinking peat; the little rills, draining the fells and winding and leaping into the valleys, turned to floods and drenched everything; the wind moaned in the brown heather in sympathy with the people. The rain reduced the working days from six a week to three or two, and the men left for other parts of the country where the weather and the work were more settled.

— Terry Coleman, The Railway Navvies (1965)

This line, since the first sod was cut at Anley in 1869, has been a roaring trail of shanty towns. Here the old English navvy, whose race will pass with the nineteenth century, has plied his pick, tipped his barrow, smashed the face of his enemy, sported his fancy waistcoat of a Sunday, lost it and everything else save his shirt, breeches and boots at crown-and-anchor on Monday night, and fallen to afresh on the last great main line to the Border, every week of the 5½ years between November 1869 and the summer of 1875.

— C. Hamilton Ellis, The Trains We Loved (1947)

ACCIDENTS

ALMOST as if the Pennine gods have resented the intrusion of their domain, the Settle & Carlisle has been blessed with more than its fair share of death and disaster. Below are listed the more serious accidents involving passenger trains:

August 15th, 1876 Ormside

First significant accident on line. Down goods train became divided and then derailed, up passenger train colliding with some of the wagons. Two passengers and guard injured.

June 26th, 1878 Settle Junction

Driver of up goods mis-read signals and collided with Morecambe–Leeds passenger train. Six passengers injured.

August 19th, 1880 Blea Moor tunnel

A near escape from major disaster. Leeds–Carlisle train stopped in tunnel owing to brake failure. Signalman's error allowed St. Pancras–Glasgow train to proceed into tunnel, but driver heard detonators put down by guard of failed train and managed to reduce speed to 10mph. Minor impact took place — no passenger injuries.

July 12th, 1888 Crosby Garrett

Seven passengers and inspector injured when excursion train ran into buffer stop as it was being set back into siding.

July 22nd, 1891 Hawes Junction

As a result of station-master giving incorrect instructions, Bradford–Aysgarth excursion set back into dead-end siding with great force. Eighteen passengers injured.

December 24th, 1910 Hawes Junction

The first major disaster on the line — and one that for high drama has few equals. On a wild Pennine night, the Hawes Junction signalman forgot two Carlisle-bound light engines standing on the down main line. Their drivers did nothing to remind him of their presence, and after almost 15 minutes eased their engines out of the station when the signals came off for a down express. They had only just crossed Lunds viaduct when the double-headed passenger train bore down on them at 65mph. In the resulting derailment and fire, twelve passengers died and nine were injured.

September 2nd, 1913 Ais Gill

Less than three years later occurred the line's worst accident of all in terms of passenger fatalities — 16 died and 38 were injured. An up night sleeper stalled just half a mile short of Ais Gill summit owing to overloading and poor coal. The following train was also having steaming problems which caused the crew to run through all the Mallerstang signals. A rear-end collision and fire ensued.

January 19th, 1918 Little Salkeld

Down express ran into massive landslide in Long Meg cutting, brought on by sudden thaw. Two leading coaches were violently telescoped and seven passengers killed.

March 6th, 1930 Culgaith

Combination of errors led to head-on collision between down stopping train and ballast train on wrong line. One passenger later died in hospital.

April 18th, 1952 Blea Moor

'Thames–Clyde Express' became derailed at speed on facing points of up loop, due to brake rod on pilot engine coming adrift and damaging track. Twenty-nine passengers injured.

January 21st, 1960 Settle

The most recent major accident on the line — again at night in appalling weather conditions. Piston rod on locomotive of up night sleeper fractured and drove into the ballast, just as a Leeds–Carlisle goods was passing. The goods engine immediately slewed across the down line and sliced into the coaches of the express. Five passengers killed and nine injured.

having as its only approach a corkscrew road climbing 450ft in little more than half a mile. It is followed by Rise Hill, the second of the two major tunnels on the route, taking the line on to another ledge, this time above the straight and not-so-green Garsdale. A remote stretch of railway, this is a fitting location for the world's highest water troughs which for many years were steam-heated against frost. Garsdale station, until 1959 junction for the Hawes branch, was in its heyday a self-contained railway community with several rows of cottages and a social centre under the water tank! Its most famous feature was a stockaded turntable, the encircling row of upright sleepers being erected after an engine was caught by a freak wind and sent whirling round like a spinning top. Only a short distance to the north is the line's summit at lonely Ais Gill, 1,169ft above sea level.

The descent begins almost immediately, the tracks running along a ledge above evocatively-named Mallerstang and below the impressive 2,342ft bulk of Wild Boar Fell before disappearing into Birkett tunnel, less than ¼-mile long but passing through shale, limestone, grit, slate, ironstone, coal and lead! The tunnel marks the beginning of kinder terrain with the bleak Pennine wastes left behind and the fertile Eden Valley stretching away to the north. Somewhat surprisingly, it is on the less spectacular stretch of line north of Kirkby Stephen that the highest viaduct on the Midland Railway is found at Smardale, towering 131ft above Scandal Beck and until 1962 having the Barnard Castle–Tebay line passing under one of its twelve arches. It is the last of the really major engineering works on the route, although northwards there are still numerous tunnels and viaducts which on any other line would be considered outstanding features. Beyond Appleby there is a particularly attractive stretch between Lazonby and Cotehill, with the tracks running through the thickly wooded Eden gorge above the winding river, but all too soon the railway which has successfully challenged mountains makes what by comparison seems a very tame approach to Carlisle and quietly loses its identity in a maze of points and crossings.

The most glorious years of the Settle–Carlisle railway coincided with England's so-called golden age in the palmy Edwardian era of the early 1900s. Midland red ran proudly over Ais Gill with rolling stock that was second to none, cocking a snoot at both the smug 'Premier Line' from Euston and the ill-assorted East Coast companies. Many were the passengers who were wooed by the Midland's plush comfort and vigorous advertising to "Choose Aye the Middle Course — the Most Interesting Route to Scotland".

The amount of passenger traffic over the line was in vivid contrast to that of today. Imagine a summer afternoon at Hawes Junction in say 1904, when the station would have been a railway enthusiast's paradise. At 12.36 the branch train from Hawes arrived, to be followed five minutes later by a Carlisle–Hellifield slow which shunted to permit an Edinburgh to London and Bristol express to run through at one o'clock. Subsequent five minute intervals saw the departure of the branch train to Hawes, and then the arrival of an express from Glasgow to Manchester, London and Bristol which called in order to make a connection with the Hellifield slow. This last finally got away at 1.16, after which there was a lull until a Manchester, Liverpool and London express ran through in separate portions from Aberdeen/Edinburgh and Glasgow at 2.25 and 2.40.

A quarter of an hour later came the first of the down London day expresses — to Edinburgh and Aberdeen — followed by a Hellified–Carlisle slow which stood by for twenty minutes to allow the passage of a London–Glasgow express. The stopping train pulled out at 3.25, ten minutes after a branch service to Hawes. Another respite preceded a forty minute period from 4.35 to 5.15 which brought a Carlisle–Hellifield slow, an express from London, Bristol, Manchester and Liverpool running in separate portions to Glasgow and Edinburgh/Aberdeen, a Glasgow–London express and a Hellifield–Carlisle semi-fast. And so the pattern continued into the late evening, with two expresses stopping only to set down passengers from Carlisle and Scotland. Finally, in the long and often wild hours of darkness came the night sleepers conveying through coaches to such evocative destinations as Stranraer, Fort William and Inverness.

Many of these trains would be handled by the famous 'Compounds' which arrived on the line in 1902 and soon became a familiar sight, being built by Samuel Johnson, his successor Richard Deeley and, after the Grouping, by the London, Midland & Scottish Railway.

It took a long time for the LMS to evolve locomotive policy, a major problem being the rivalry which still smouldered between ex London & North Western and Midland factions in the new establishment. One of the many waves of discontent erupted on the Settle–Carlisle line when, to the horror of former Midland drivers, the 'Compounds' were replaced by L&NW 'Claughtons'. But with the appointment of Sir William Stanier as locomotive superintendent, profound changes eventually came in the 1930s. The 'Patriots', 'Jubilees' and 'Black Fives', all of the 4–6–0 wheel arrangement, were introduced within a short space of years and the 'Claughtons' disappeared from the scene.

During the second world war traffic over the line became even heavier, and so bridges were strengthened in order to accommodate the powerful 'Scot' class 4–6–0s which made their debut in 1943. These handled the bulk of the expresses until 1960, when steam passenger working on the Settle–Carlisle reached its greatest variety as it stood on the brink of dissolution. In 1961 some of Gresley's A3 Pacifics, displaced by dieselisation on the East Coast route, began to work over Ais Gill from Holbeck shed. They put up some fine performances and, with British Railways 4–6–2 'Britannias' and 'Clans' also in regular use, the line provided a marvellous stomping ground for the student of locomotive performance.

On the freight side virtually all traffic from opening until the late 1920s was handled by the ubiquitous 0–6–0, which was turned out in the hundred by both the Midland and LMS railways. After the Grouping some ex Glasgow & South Western Railway 2–6–0s were tried over the line, and these were followed by Sir Henry Fowler's class 5F 2–6–0s. In the late 1930s Stanier's mixed-traffic 'Black Five' 4–6–0s and 8F 2–8–0s were introduced and formed the mainstay of freight working until the latter days of steam operation. Finally, the 9F 2–10–0s provided a fitting epilogue to the story of steam traction on the Settle–Carlisle. One will long remember them, all smoke and glory, as they roused the echoes in Mallerstang or trundled quietly over Arten Gill in the dusky shadows of a Dentdale evening.

One of the great days in Settle–Carlisle history occurred on August 11th, 1968, when traffic jams formed at Ais Gill and Ribblehead as the faithful arrived by the hundreds to witness the passage of a pair of 'Black Fives' on what was proclaimed as 'the last steam train on British Railways'. The high Pennines had never seen anything quite like it before, yet the atmosphere was inevitably one of overwhelming sadness. It was the end of an era — or so it seemed.

Rain clouds gather over Ribblehead as a WD 2–8–0 on a down freight trundles north over the twenty-four arches towards Blea Moor.
(October 1965) ***(A. E. R. Cope)***

TICKET
OFFICE
BEWARE
OF
TRAINS
70035

Right: No smokeless zone over Appleby as stoker-fired 9F No. 92167 pounds up-gradient with a Carlisle–Water Orton freight.
(July 1961) *(Derek Cross/Colour-Rail)*

Left: Dramatic evening sunshine highlights 'Britannia' No. 70035 *Rudyard Kipling* leaving Garsdale with a stopping train from Carlisle.
(August 1964)
(A. E. R. Cope/Colour-Rail)

Right: Jets of steam issuing from the tender show that the coal-pusher is in use as 'Britannia' No. 70045, formerly named *Lord Rowallan*, storms up the 'Long Drag' near Selside.
(April 1967)
(M. Chapman/Colour-Rail)

Dent Head, perhaps the most majestically situated of all the Settle & Carlisle viaducts, is crossed by a 5MT in charge of some forty assorted goods vans.
(May 1966) ***(A. E. R. Cope)***

A begrimed 'Britannia' — in the last few months of its life — leans to the curve on the approach to Dent station with a down goods.
(June 1966) *(A. E. R. Cope/Colour-Rail)*

5MT No. 44884 heads south from Blea Moor tunnel past the flanks of Whernside with a rake of empty coaching stock.
(June 1965) *(A. E. R. Cope)*

The characteristic mixed-train formation of a Settle & Carlisle stopping service is seen coming off Ribblehead viaduct behind 'Scot' No. 46115 *Scots Guardsman.*
(August 1965)
(M. Chapman/Colour-Rail)

Far from home, Great Western Railway No. 7029 *Clun Castle* heads through Armathwaite with an enthusiasts' special. This locomotive is now preserved at the Birmingham Railway Museum at Tyseley.
(October 14th, 1967) *(A. E. R. Cope)*

An up freight — with the kind of varied make-up that is now rarely seen — breasts Ais Gill summit behind a 5MT 4–6–0 fitted with a buffer-beam snowplough.
(1967) *(Peter J. Robinson)*

3.
The Diesel Age

The Diesel Age

DIESEL locomotives took over the most of the Settle & Carlisle's express passenger workings in 1962/3, some five years before the end of steam. They got off to a rough start in one of the worst winters on record. At about 3am on January 20th, 1963, the Edinburgh–London sleeper hauled by a Type 4 became stranded in a drift just south of Rise Hill tunnel. Fortunately it was possible to transfer all the passengers to the rear three coaches and, after the line had been cleared by plough, a heroic crew worked these back to Carlisle with an engine running tender first into the teeth of the blizzard. The line was blocked for a further five days, all trains following the now abandoned diversion route via Ingleton and Low Gill until they were allowed to nudge past the towering drifts at Dent.

The coming of the diesels coincided with the onset of the Settle & Carlisle's age of uncertainty. Enthusiasts watched with growing dismay at what seemed to be a systematic dismemberment of the line's lifeblood, a process that began with abandonment of the Hawes branch in 1959. Policy statements of the 1960s proposed that all passenger services be withdrawn and the line reduced to two 'sidings' to serve the mineral workings at either end, through traffic being diverted on to an electrified West Coast route at either Preston or Carnforth. As a result maintenance was cut to a minimum, speed restrictions enforced and the whole line began to take on an air of neglect. Many stations had already been closed, while annual ticket sales along the route had shrunk from a peak of 150,000 at the turn of the century to 35,000. A proposal to withdraw local services and close all remaining stations apart from Settle and Appleby was refused by the Minister of Transport in 1964 on the grounds of hardship, and matters seemed to be taking a turn for the better when diesel multiple-unit 'paytrains' were introduced in April 1966. It proved a short-lived reprieve, the closure proposals being implemented in May 1970 even though the North West Area of the Transport Users' Consultative Committee had stated that 'severe or very severe hardship' would be caused to local people, as well as considerable inconvenience to travellers from other areas who used the stations for access to the Yorkshire Dales National Park. Goods facilities had been withdrawn from all stations by 1971.

Yet even in what looked like terminal illness, there were signs of revival. Settle began to be served by expresses for the first time in its history. More and more people became aware of the scenic splendours of England's highest main line, and the number of special workings increased year by year. Electrification of the West Coast Route saw processions of diverted traffic pounding over Ais Gill. Ironically, it was this work which finally brought a change in the fortunes of the Settle & Carlisle. The difficulty of interlacing slow freight trains with 100mph electric-hauled expresses became fully realised, and it was evident that at the then traffic levels the Midland route would have to be retained for freight and diversionary purposes. Thus, on the eve of its centenary, the Settle & Carlisle entered a new era and began to

THE KEY DATES

10 May 1844	Midland Railway formed.
16 July 1866	Act authorising construction of Settle & Carlisle Railway receives royal assent.
November 1869	First sod of line cut at Anley House, near Settle.
2 August 1875	Line opened for freight traffic.
1 May 1876	Line opened for passenger traffic.
1 August 1878	Hawes branch opened for freight traffic.
1 October 1878	Hawes branch opened for passenger traffic.
1 January 1923	Midland Railway vested in London Midland & Scottish Railway.
1 January 1948	LMS vested in British Railways.
16 March 1959	Hawes branch closed to all traffic.
2 January 1967	Surviving intermediate stations — except Settle and Appleby — become unstaffed halts.
4 May 1970	Stopping passenger services withdrawn and all stations except Settle and Appleby closed.
3 May 1975	Dales Rail service inaugurated, with reopening of intermediate stations between Settle and Appleby on selected weekends.
25 March 1978	Steam specials commence to run over line.
17 May 1982	Nottingham–Glasgow Inter-City services diverted away from line and replaced by Leeds–Carlisle trains.
18 August 1983	British Rail announces proposed withdrawal of passenger services and complete closure between Ribblehead and Appleby.

assume an appearance it had not enjoyed for more than a decade. Massive arrears of maintenance were tackled, track relaid, colour-light signals installed and speed restrictions lifted.

Symbolising the changed climate was the success of 'Dales Rail', a collaboration between British Rail and the Yorkshire Dales National Park Committee which in the summer of 1975 saw the reopening of several stations on higher reaches of the line for weekend 'charter' trains between Leeds and Appleby. The fare structure was designed to encourage visitors to travel into the National Park by rail instead of road and, as additional attractions, guided walks were provided from several of the stations and connecting bus services put on from Garsdale to the Sedbergh and Hawes areas. A return working enabled local residents deprived of public transport facilities five years earlier to have a day out in Leeds. A total of more than 10,000 passenger journeys were made during the twelve days of the service, which had an operating surplus. During 1976 'Dales Rail' trains also ran from Manchester, Preston and Colne, and the Saturday service was extended to Carlisle with additional stations being reopened in the Eden Valley.

Contrary to gloomy predictions of only a few years earlier, England's highest and most spectacular main line had achieved its centenary. On May 1st, 1976 — a day which perhaps appropriately was extremely cold, wet and windy — special trains and vintage rolling stock converged on Settle for celebrations culminating in a grand banquet.

By this time British Rail had reversed its rigid policy which had prevailed since 1968 and certain preserved steam locomotives were now allowed to run on a limited number of routes. Strenuous efforts were made to add the Settle & Carlisle to the approved list for the centenary, but it was not to be — one of the official reasons being the presence of overhead electrification at Carlisle. Yet two locomotives were allowed to run to the southern end of the line at Settle, where, to the delight of thousands who braved the weather, they remained simmering away in the siding for most of the afternoon. They were an ironic pair, ex London & North Western Railway No. 790 *Hardwicke* and London & North Eastern A3 No. 4472 *Flying Scotsman*, in effect representing the two pioneer Anglo–Scottish routes that had provoked the Settle & Carlisle into being. At the end of it all they puffed quietly away down-bank to Settle Junction and Hellifield — and the line reverted to the humdrum existence of the diesel age.

Eden gorge at Armathwaite.

Further Reading

THE sudden upsurge of interest in the Settle & Carlisle has brought with it a new wave of literature so vast that the newcomer to the subject can feel overwhelmed. The following details are an attempt to chart a way through what may seem to be overcrowded waters:

The most informative book is *North of Leeds: The Leeds–Settle–Carlisle Line and its Branches,* Peter E. Baughan (Roundhouse, 1966), almost a quarter of a million words setting the route in its full historical context. Possibly the most readable is *The Story of the Settle–Carlisle Line,* Frederick W. Houghton & W. Hubert Foster (Norman Arch, 1948), the pioneer work with its evocative prose and photographs. Unfortunately both are now out of print.

Providing a concise summary of all aspects of the line is *Settle to Carlisle: A Railway over the Pennines,* W. R. Mitchell & David Joy (Dalesman, 1984), a work that has gone through many previous editions. There is much stimulating content — especially visual — in *Rails in the Fells,* David Jenkinson (Peco, 1973), in the words of its sub-title 'an account of the origins, characteristics and contribution of a railway to the landscape, together with an attempt to evaluate its past and present influence on the area through which it passes'. The same author wrote the text for *Settle–Carlisle Railway Centenary 1876–1976* (British Rail, 1976), the first publication on the line to make extensive use of colour. This approach was later developed by David Joy in *Settle–Carlisle in Colour* (Dalesman, 1983).

The most useful work on the Hawes branch is *The Wensleydale Railway,* C. S. Hallas (Dalesman, 1984), which is especially strong on the social and economic history. See also *Railways in the Yorkshire Dales,* K. Hoole (Dalesman, 2nd edition 1978).

Works on the company which brought the Settle–Carlisle into being include *The Midland Railway,* C. Hamilton Ellis (Ian Allan, 1952); *Midland Style,* George Dow (Historical Model Railway Society, 1975); and the two-volume study by E. G. Barnes, *The Rise of the Midland Railway 1844–1874* and *The Midland Main Line 1875–1922* (Allen & Unwin, 1966/9).

The classic *The Midland Railway: Its Rise and Progress* by Frederick S. Williams, originally published in 1876 and reprinted by David & Charles in 1968, includes a chapter which gives the best contemporary account of the construction of the line. This theme is taken up by W. R. Mitchell in *The Long Drag: A Story of Men under stress during the construction of the Settle–Carlisle Line* (Author, 1962); *The Railway Shanties* (Settle & District Civic Society, 1975); and, with N. J. Mussett *Seven Years Hard: Building the Settle–Carlisle Railway* (Dalesman, 1976).

The same author has looked at the broader-based human story of the line in *Life on the Settle–Carlisle Railway: Anecdotes collected from railwaymen and their families* (Dalesman, 1984). In similar vein is *Ganger, Guard and Signalman: Working Memories of the Settle & Carlisle,* Dick Fawcett (Bradford Barton, 1981).

Dales Rail: A Guide to the scenic rail journey between Leeds and Carlisle (Yorkshire Dales National Park, 1976) is a brochure with pictorial maps. Official publications on the same subject are *An Opinion Survey of the Yorkshire Dales Rail Service in 1975,* A. O. Grigg & P. G. Smith (Transport and Road Research Laboratory, 1977) and *Dales Rail: A report of an experimental project in the Yorkshire Dales National Park* (Countryside Commission, 1979). The most recent report on the line, referred to extensively in this present book and simply entitled *The Settle and Carlisle Railway,* is published by PEIDA, Planning & Economic Consultants, 10 Chester Street, Edinburgh EH3 7RA.

Several more general works have a chapter specifically devoted to the Settle & Carlisle, as in O. S. Nock's *Main Lines across the Border* (Nelson, 1960; Ian Allan, 1982), the respective editions featuring some of the best photographs of Eric Treacy and Derek Cross. Another instance is *A Regional History of the Railways of Great Britain: The Lake Counties,* David Joy (David & Charles, 1983).

There have been numerous picture books: the following list — by no means exhaustive — is in order of publication: *The Steam Railway: Over the Pennine Fells,* Colin Walker (Oxford Illustrators, 1972); *Settle–Carlisle Centenary,* David Joy & W. R. Mitchell (Dalesman, 1976); *On the Settle & Carlisle Route,* T. G. Flinders (Ian Allan, 1981); *Steam on the Settle & Carlisle,* David Joy (Dalesman, 1981); *Diesels over the Settle to Carlisle Route,* Peter Walton (Oxford Publishing Co., 1982); *The Scenic Settle & Carlisle Railway,* Donald Binns (Wyvern, 1982); and *Settle & Carlisle Railway Twilight Years,* David T. Roberts (Wyvern, 1984).

Finally, two novels feature the railway. Graham Sutton's *Fleming of Honister* (Hodder & Stoughton, 1953) centres on the fortunes of John Fleming, a quarryman, who leaves Borrowdale for work on the line in the Eden Valley. *Hills of Sheep* by Emmeline Garnett (Hodder & Stoughton, 1955) is a story for children about the friendship of a small boy from Gearstones with the engineer Sharland and a navvy family from Blea Moor.

The Video Age

POSTERITY may take the view that the video arrived just in time to capture the Settle & Carlisle. Certainly, as with books, there have been plenty of recent productions:

Steam on the Settle & Carlisle, Border Television, 1983, 26 minutes.
An absolute gem, professionally produced to the standards that only a television film crew can achieve. This award-winning film, with its inspiring music and excellent helicopter work, concentrates on 'Sir Nigel Gresley' hauling the Cumbrian Mountain Express over the northern stretch of the line between Carlisle and Ais Gill.

A Driver's Eye View of the Settle & Carlisle Railway, Video 125, 1984, 60 minutes.
Far better than it sounds, with high-quality filming and informative commentary adding interest to the inch-by-inch view from the cab which captures the majesty of the line in a way that no carriage window can emulate.

The Settle & Carlisle Railway, Cresswell Video, 60 minutes.
In two parts, the first 'Rails Across the Fells' putting the line in its historical perspective by means of video, cine, stills and an excellent commentary. The second and longer part features sequences of passing trains ranging from steam specials to diesel-hauled freights.

Steam over the Settle to Carlisle Railway, 3D's Video Library, 1984.
Concentrates entirely on steam-hauled specials, including virtually all the trains that ran in 1983.

British Steam Cavalcade — part 2, Nick Lera Video Collection, 1983, 45 minutes.
Lengthy sequences of preserved steam locomotives at Ribblehead, Dent Head, Garsdale and Ais Gill. Displays a high degree of professionalism.

There are others, aimed mainly at the locomotive enthusiast, and the range is rapidly expanding. Additions are advertised in the various railway magazines, which in 1984 carried considerable correspondence about the deplorable standard of many videos. Be warned!

The Midland Board resolved that it was its duty, single-handed, to find a way by a middle route — the only possible one that nature had left. How long and arduous was the conflict, both in Parliament and out, and then with the stupendous natural obstacles of the country it had to surmount, we have not time to tell. I shall never forget as long as I live the difficulties that surrounded us in that undertaking. If I had one work in my life that gave me more anxiety than another, it was the Settle–Carlisle line.

James Allport, General Manager, Midland Railway (1880)

Magnificent in both concept and execution it is somewhat surprising to find that in both time and cost the Midland Railway seriously underestimated the difficulties of construction. Nowadays it is considerably easier to gain access to the Dales, but anyone who has stayed for even a week in a holiday cottage, tried to repair a slightly damaged stone wall, walked across a waterlogged field or even attempted to walk a few hundred yards in any of the extreme conditions of weather which occur in these northern climes would define the task of building a railway through such terrain as 'impossible'.

T. G. Flinders, On the Settle & Carlisle Route (1981)

It is distinguished by its straightness. It meant to get to Scotland in the fastest possible time and would brook no delays. If a hill got in the way, the Settle–Carlisle went straight through it — either by tunnel or cutting! It has nineteen viaducts and fourteen tunnels. Its viaducts are titanic examples of Victorian architecture, built by men who clearly believed that while the impossible might take a little longer it had better not take too long!

— "A Century of Settle–Carlisle" (Yorkshire Life, 1976)

A pair of class 25s headed by No. 25154 approach Dent with a block cement train — note the remnants of the snow fences on the left of the picture.
(1976) ***(J. Winkley)***

Left: The deep cutting north of Dent station dwarfs class 45 No. 45013 on an up freight.
(1976) *(J. Winkley)*

Right: Class 31 No. 31407 approaches Crosby Garrett with the afternoon Carlisle–Leeds train.
(June 29th, 1983) *(Gavin Morrison)*

Left: A class 45 — in its original guise as a green-liveried 'Peak' — rushes through Dent station with the up Thames–Clyde Express.
(May 1966) *(A. E. R. Cope)*

The rare sight of a High Speed Train on the Settle–Carlisle, seen at Baron Wood on a return Leeds–Armathwaite run to provide B.R. publicity photographs.
(October 24th, 1981) *(Mrs D. A. Robinson)*

A six-car diesel unit climbs out of the Eden Valley at Birkett Common with a return Appleby–Derby ramblers' excursion.
(August 29th, 1983) ***(Mrs D. A. Robinson)***

In the last week of through Glasgow–Nottingham services over the line, class 47 No. 47451 passes through Baron Wood, near Armathwaite, with the afternoon train.
(May 10th, 1982) (Mrs D. A. Robinson)

Sunday diversions of West Coast main line trains have been a regular feature of Settle–Carlisle operations for many years. Here class 47 No. 47460 is seen leaving Dandry Mire viaduct to enter Garsdale with the 8.25am Glasgow–Euston express.
(March 30th, 1980) ***(Mrs D. A. Robinson)***

One of the busiest weekends on the Settle–Carlisle was Easter 1983 when the West Coast route was closed for some 60 hours for a bridge renewal at Tebay. Class 40s Nos. 40082 and 40129 were placed on stand-by at Blea Moor in case of locomotive failure on a diverted train.
(April 2nd, 1983) *(Gavin Morrison)*

4.

Return of Steam

Return of Steam

LESS than two years after the diesel-dominated centenary celebrations, British Rail changed its mind and agreed to a limited return of steam specials over the Settle & Carlisle in 1978. It was just one of the many surprises that the line has produced in recent times — although only a few years earlier such a development would have seemed beyond the wildest dreams. The railway that had become one of the great survivors, clinging on to life against seemingly insuperable odds, was now entering a new era as one of the most splendid of all settings to see preserved steam locomotives at work in weather both fair and — more usually — foul.

Alas, on the first return of steam to the route in March 1978 the Pennine weather, true to form, conspired to produce its worst and LNER 4771 *Green Arrow* was glimpsed hurrying across the viaduct like a shadow, against the misty 'white-out' of driving snow. Nevertheless the sight and sound of steam was back on the 'Long Drag'. Some weeks later saw the BR 9F *Evening Star,* No. 92220, hauling another special over the line on May 13th, 1978. Sadly, one of the finest of railway photographers and Settle–Carlisle enthusiast, Bishop Eric Treacy, died at Appleby station whilst awaiting this special. As a tribute to this man BR ran two steam specials in his honour on September 30th, 1978 and named them 'The Lord Bishop' and 'The Bishop Treacy'.

Further complications arose in 1979. As a result of the diversions necessitated over the line because of the tunnel collapse at Penmanshiel on the East Coast main line, the planned steam specials for that year were cancelled for the Settle–Carlisle route.

Then in the early months of 1980, thanks to the tireless efforts of the Steam Locomotive Operators' Association (SLOA) and the co-operation of British Rail, a train to be called the Cumbrian Mountain Express was introduced to run both north and south over the Settle–Carlisle line, using the electrified route of the west coast to complete the circular tour. This eventually produced more steam on the line than since its closure to steam in 1968. Truly a 'second coming' had dawned for steam and the Settle–Carlisle. Originally there were to be six trains, three northbound and three southbound between January 19th and March 22nd, 1980. Demand was so great in fact, that the number of trains run was doubled and the workings continued until Saturday, April 19th, finally culminating the following weekend, April 26th, with a return run on the one day by LMS 'Jubilee' 5690 *Leander.*

Typically these days and runs enabled the photographer to sample the best and worst of the weather in the high fells, and one cannot but feel that the inhabitants of the dales must have become quite used to the weekly influx of enthusiasts on Saturdays.

The Cumbrian Mountain Express ran in two 'legs', first from Carnforth to Skipton and then Skipton to Carlisle, northbound, and the following week in reverse order, southbound, with the steam locomotive being 'shedded' at Carlisle for the intervening week. The ex-LMS 'Black 5' No. 5305, in superb condition, from Mr. Draper at Hull, ran on no less than ten of these first Cumbrian Mountain Expresses. This was surely fitting for this ex-LMS route. Ex-LNER No. 4472 *Flying Scotsman* and 4498 *Sir Nigel Gresley* shared the journeys with 5305, whilst ex-LMS

VIADUCTS

Miles*	Name	Length (yards)	Height (feet)	Arches
5¾	Sheriff Brow	58	55	3
6	Ribble	55	25	3
13	Ribblehead	440	104	24
16½	Dent Head	199	100	10
17½	Arten Gill	220	117	11
22¼	Dandry Mire	227	50	12
23	Lunds	103	63	5
26	Ais Gill	87	75	4
34	Smardale	237	131	12
34¾	Crosby Garrett	110	55	6
37	Griseburn	142	74	7
40½	Ormside	200	90	10
45	Long Marton	108	60	5
49	Crowdundle	86	55	4
54¾	Little Salkeld	134	60	7
56½	Eden Lacy	137	60	7
62½	Armathwaite	176	80	9
64½	Dry Beck	139	80	7
66	High Stand Gill	91	60	4

* from Settle Junction.

'Jubilee' No. 5690 *Leander* ran on the last two of the winter Cumbrian Mountain Expresses. All these locomotives put up some sterling and memorable performances. Apart from the normal stops necessitated by locomotive changes, the CME tours allowed photographic stops at Dent, Garsdale, and Appleby, northbound, and at Appleby and Garsdale, southbound. Such was the locomotive performance on the early tours that a southbound stop was soon added at Ribblehead and one at Armathwaite northbound.

Such was the success of the winter CMEs that BR decided to run Cumbrian Mountain Expresses during the summer months of 1980, southbound only as a tourist service for the general public rather than especially for the enthusiast. This was to be a complementary service to the already well-proven Cumbrian Coast Express. The locomotive from the CCE upon arrival at Ravenglass worked on to Carlisle and then two days later hauled the CME from Carlisle to Skipton; another steam locomotive then completed the journey from Skipton to Carnforth. In addition to LNER 4472, LNER 4498 and LMS 5690, Steamtown included ex-SR 850 *Lord Nelson*. 850 was hastily restored to main-line running order just in time for the 'Rocket 150' celebrations in May 1980 and from then onwards the 'Lord' showed his paces over the 'Long Drag' on several of the summer 1980 Cumbrian Mountain Expresses. Ex-LMS 4–6–2 6201 *Princess Elizabeth* also spent a few weeks among the 'royalty' at Steamtown during the summer and hauled the CME upon a couple of occasions. Although only southbound trains were run the CMEs were well patronised by the public, despite the indifferent summer weather.

Encouraged by the success of the 1980 CME tours over the Settle–Carlisle line, British Rail and the SLOA arranged a programme of 1980/81 winter CMEs. Not as many were planned or actually run as in 1980, because SLOA diversified, introducing the 'Welsh Marches Express' on the alternate Saturdays to the CME. Nevertheless, the 1981 winter CMEs involved different and interesting locomotives, including two ex-LMS Black Fives, Stanier's mixed traffic design, 4767 and 5407. 4767 *George Stephenson* came down to Steamtown from the North Yorkshire Moors Railway to join 5407; both were resplendent in different LMS liveries, 5407 in pre-war lined black and 4767 in the post-war black livery. These two were joined by another famous ex-LMS locomotive, the 'Pacific' 4–6–2 46229 *Duchess of Hamilton* restored in crimson BR livery. Unfortunately the weather was not too kind on the days when the 'Duchess' hauled the CMEs but she made a memorable sight as, clad in rich maroon, she climbed from the green backcloth of the Ribble valley up into the browns, russets, purples and greys of the high fells and moorlands of Blea Moor and Wild Boar Fell and then down into the lush greens of the Eden valley.

Poetic justice occurred, some may say, when on her first northbound run 46229 had to be assisted at the rear of the train by a Class 40 because of lack of adhesion due to greasy, autumn leaf-covered rails! The final winter northbound CME was double-headed by the 'Black Fives' 4767 and 5407. Some spectacular exhaust patterns were produced by this pair, especially on the climb over Ribblehead. One other innovation occurred during the running of the winter CMEs; this was the introduction by BR of 'run pasts'. This allowed the passengers on the CME to disembark, suitably position themselves and then take photographs of the locomotive and train in action. These 'run pasts' have usually taken place at Appleby, Garsdale and, more recently, Ribblehead. In all cases the fireman responded to the call by coaling up the fire, which produced some rich, claggy, high skybound combinations of smoke and steam.

In April 1981, SLOA purchased a train of Pullman coaches and the last winter CME used these coaches and became instead the first Cumbrian Mountain Pullman. 5407 hauled this train from Carlisle to Skipton, complete with some spectacular run pasts, in a style well worthy of this former LMS locomotive.

Three years from their inception, steam specials over the Settle & Carlisle were by now both well-established and consistently popular. The winter 1982 programme saw two ex Southern Railway locomotives join the group of engines passed for performance over the route. During December 1981, SR Pacific 4–6–2 *City of Wells*, No. 34092, was tested for main line

TUNNELS

Miles*	Name	Length (yards)	Height above sea level (feet)	Date completed
4	Taitlands	120	620	?
15	Blea Moor	2629	1140	1875
20	Rise Hill	1213	1140	1875
22¾	Moorcock	98	1120	1874
23¾	Shotlock Hill	106	1150	1874
30	Birkett	424	960	1874
34¼	Crosby Garrett	181	740	1875
38½	Helm	571	600	1873
50½	Culgaith	661	380	1873
50¾	Waste Bank	164	380	?
57½	Lazonby	99	300	1872
61	Baron Wood No 1	207	330	1873
61¼	Baron Wood No 2	251	320	1873
62	Armathwaite	325	300	1871

* from Settle Junction.

running on the Leeds–Carnforth line, with great success. Thus it came about that on February 6th, 1982, 34092 left Keighley from her home on the Keighley and Worth Valley Railway and steamed to Hellifield to pick up the northbound CMP. Typically enough, the Pennine gods provided high winds and heavy rain with much low cloud, making it a very poor day for photography.

STATIONS

Miles*		Opened	Closed Passengers	Closed Goods
0	Settle Junction	10 Nov 1876	1 Nov 1877	1 Nov 1877
2	Settle	1 May 1876		12 Oct 1970
8	Horton-in-Ribblesdale *	1 May 1876	4 May 1970	1 Feb 1965
12¾	Ribblehead *	4 Dec 1876	4 May 1970	7 Nov 1966
18¾	Dent *	6 Aug 1877	4 May 1970	1 Oct 1964
22	Garsdale * (originally Hawes Junction)	1 Aug 1876	4 May 1970	6 Apr 1964
32	Kirkby Stephen *	1 May 1876	4 May 1970	28 Sep 1964
35¼	Crosby Garrett	1 May 1876	6 Oct 1952	6 Oct 1952
40¼	Ormside	1 May 1876	2 Jun 1952	2 Jun 1952
42¾	Appleby	1 May 1876		18 Oct 1971
45½	Long Marton	1 May 1876	4 May 1970	6 Apr 1964
48¾	Newbiggin	1 May 1876	4 May 1970	7 Nov 1966
50¼	Culgaith	1 Apr 1880	4 May 1970	5 Oct 1964
53½	Langwathby †	1 May 1876	4 May 1970	6 Jul 1964
55	Little Salkeld	1 May 1876	4 May 1970	6 Jul 1964
58	Lazonby †	1 May 1876	4 May 1970	2 Nov 1964
63½	Armathwaite †	1 May 1876	4 May 1970	6 Apr 1964
66¾	Cotehill	1 May 1876	7 Apr 1952	7 Apr 1952
69½	Cumwhinton	1 May 1876	5 Nov 1956	5 Nov 1956
70¾	Scotby	1 May 1876	1 Feb 1942	1 Feb 1942

* reopened for Dales Rail services 1975.
† reopened for Dales Rail services 1976.

Yet the following Saturday the sun shone as 34092 departed from Carlisle about midday.

By March, after many setbacks another ex-SR locomotive was ready for main line work. 4–6–0 No. 777 *Sir Lamiel* was restored in SR green livery by the Humberside Group at Hull to the same excellent standards that they had restored the 'Black Five' No. 5305. Nevertheless, for the inaugural run over the Long Drag, British Rail decided it would be safer to assist *Sir Lamiel*. So, 777 was coupled with 'Black Five' 5407 for both the north and southbound runs. In sunny weather, 777 proved to be yet another fine performer on this scenic route. The winter was cold, though not as severe as some on the Settle–Carlisle, but the water servicing at Garsdale was unusable because of frozen and broken pipes. As a result the Cumbrian Mountain Pullman's locomotives took on water from a road tanker parked on the accommodation bridge at Ais Gill instead of at Garsdale station.

After a successful winter season, the SLOA expresses continued to run on the Saturdays in May, hauled by ex-SR locomotives 34092 and 777. The spring CMPs came to a climax at Spring Bank Holiday weekend with a double-headed train hauled by ex-LMS locomotives 5407 and 'Jubilee' 5690. Many memories were evoked that weekend by the sight of the pairing — memories of the 'Thames–Clyde Express' of twenty years ago! What a pity that the coaches were not maroon to complete the picture.

Even more nostalgic was the pairing of 5690 *Leander* with the preserved Midland 'Compound' No. 1000 on February 12th, 1983, both locomotives in their maroon livery making a magnificent sight as they stormed over Ais Gill in deep snow. Each year tends to produce its own special highlight, that of 1984 in an almost literal sense occurring when another newcomer, A4 No. 60009 *Union of South Africa*, went over in magnificent style in the height of the drought. The result was a scorched earth look

The Long Drag suffers a haulage handicap not shown by the gradient-profile, and that is wind. When a train is over a thousand feet above sea level on a viaduct a hundred and fifty feet above the ground, where the fells funnel a gale across the track, a rip-roaring south-wester can transcend the most imaginative interpretation of the word 'wind'. Not only might a gale stop a train that was by its weight alone a sufficient drag on the engine, but it could trim down the coal-heap on the tender and could blow out of the lee gangway any coal that the fireman might try to feed to the fire with the shovel.

— W. A. Tuplin, Midland Steam (1973)

The most outstanding thing about the Settle to Carlisle is wind. Around here you get Helm Wind, which is local, and sometimes you can see it, a high black cloud sticking straight up in the sky; it can be bloody draughty, Helm Wind, but nowt like what you get down at Ribblehead, where I've crossed the viaduct on my hands and knees.

— Norman Greenhow, retired Appleby porter

Ribblehead viaduct is very famous for its winds. I've even seen cars blown over the side. We had several waggons loaded with them one wild night a few years back; halfway over the viaduct, there were suddenly a terrific shower of sparks and, when we got to Dent box, the signalman shouted, "Lads! Three of thy Humber Snipes is missing!" And, by God, they were. We found them at first light, just scrap metal down in the stream bed below.

— Settle–Carlisle guard

as lineside fires flared up one after another!

Thus, the spectacle of steam on the Settle & Carlisle continues. When the specials run, upwards of a thousand folk can be seen congregated by the lineside with tripods, cameras and video recorders to the fore. There can be as much entertainment in watching the faithful make the great locomotive chase from one location to another as there is in witnessing the passage of the train itself. It is not the same railway as in the early 1960s, when the only sounds to disturb the stillness of the fells as one waited for a train to come — or, more often, not come — were sheep bleating, lapwings crying and, always, the wind sighing through stunted grasses. Times have changed, but the present high drama and mass excitement is infinitely preferable to the prospect of total silence and no railway at all.

Return of steam! After an absence of almost ten years, steam made a triumphant come-back to the Settle & Carlisle early in 1978 when V2 No. 4771 *Green Arrow* headed 'The Norfolkman'. Here the special pauses before admirers at Appleby station.
(March 25th, 1978) ***(A. E. R. Cope)***

Left: The full glory of LMS passenger-engine livery as exemplified by 'Jubilee' No. 5690 *Leander* passing through Baron Wood on an up rail-tour.
(April 26th, 1980) (Mrs D. A. Robinson)

Right: One of the most delightful specials to have run over the line comprised two coaches and ex-North British 0–6–0 No. 673 *Maude*. The combination is seen at Baron Wood en route to the Liverpool & Manchester Railway 150th anniversary celebrations.
(May 17th, 1980) (Gavin Morrison)

673
NATIONAL GIROBANK

Southern Railway 4–6–0 No. 850 *Lord Nelson* at the head of 'The Wedding Belle', crossing Ribblehead viaduct with steam to spare.
(July 29th, 1981) ***(D. Morris)***

Arten Gill viaduct and its bleak surroundings totally dwarf 5MT No. 5305 hurrying northwards with the Cumbrian Mountain Express in its first months of operation.
(March 1st, 1980) ***(D. Morris)***

Left: This could so easily be LMS days! Midland Compound No. 1000 and 'Jubilee' No. 5690 *Leander* approach Ais Gill summit with the Cumbrian Mountain Pullman in the deep mid-winter snows.
(February 12th, 1983) *(John Hunt)*

Right: Ribblehead, with Wherrside providing a majestic backcloth, has proved an ideal location for photographic stops and run-pasts. 9F No. 92220 *Evening Star* poses in pristine condition before the cameras.
(April 23rd, 1984) *(Gavin Morrison)*

Left: The Gresley look. A4 No. 60009 *Union of South Africa* climbs up the 'Long Drag' out of Settle in fine style. On a later run this locomotive successfully set fire to much of the surrounding countryside!
(April 28th, 1984) *(R. Bastin)*

CUMBRIAN
MOUNTAIN
EXPRESS
92220

Au revoir! One of the finest preserved locomotives of them all, No. 46229 *Duchess of Hamilton*, catches the last of the afternoon sun as it leaves Appleby on a winter's day.
(January 1984) ***(J. Winkley)***